THE
Archive Photographs
SERIES
AROUND
OUNDLE
AND
THRAPSTON

THE
Archive Photographs
SERIES
AROUND
OUNDLE
AND
THRAPSTON

Compiled by
Peter Hill

CHALFORD

First published 1997
Copyright © Peter Hill, 1997

The Chalford Publishing Company
St Mary's Mill, Chalford,
Stroud, Gloucestershire, GL6 8NX

ISBN 0 7524 0749 X

Typesetting and origination by
The Chalford Publishing Company
Printed in Great Britain by
Redwood Books, Trowbridge

Other books by the author

(Local History)
The Archive Photographs Series: Corby
Rockingham Forest: Then and Now
In Search of the Green Man in Northamptonshire
Corby At War
A History of Great Oakley in Northamptonshire
Memories of Great Oakley
Portrait of Great Oakley

(Literature)
Sweet and Sour
Marianna
Travelines
Timepieces

Contents

Introduction

Much of the area covered in this book is known as Rockingham Forest. Like many other royal forests which came into being under William the Conqueror in the latter years of the eleventh century, it was created for the purpose of hunting, and placed under a special set of laws designed to ensure that only the king could hunt deer and boar, or cut down trees. Although the penalties for flouting these laws were, in theory, mutilation or hanging, in practice, heavy fines, imprisonment or banishment, were the norm.

When the boundaries of Rockingham Forest were first established, they stretched from near Stamford in the north, to Oxendon Bridge at Northampton in the south; the western and eastern boundaries were formed by the River Welland and the River Nene respectively. The word 'forest', incidentally, does not, or did not, mean that the land was entirely wooded - on the contrary, much of it was open countryside.

In 1299, after centuries spent petitioning successive kings, much of the area was disafforested (freed from Forest Law) allowing landowners more freedom to do as they pleased on their own land. A new perambulation was carried out and, as a result, Rockingham Forest shrank considerably, until the southern limit was just north of Kettering, and the northern limit at Duddington. This did not affect Thrapston, which, lying as it did on the other side of the Nene, had never been a forest settlement. Oundle may, or may not, have heaved a sigh of relief. On the one hand, freedom meant not having to answer a blow on the horn from the king's forester (who in medieval times acted as a kind of gamekeeper/policeman) to help him apprehend poachers, or having to provide foresters with meat and drink for themselves and their beasts. But, on the other hand, Oundle, as a forest village, had unlimited common rights, including being able to graze animals and gather naturally-fallen wood for fuel.

Of course, times have changed, but whether inside or on the edge of Rockingham Forest the towns and villages featured in this book have retained a common sense of identity that is not found elsewhere in the county.

This book focusses partly on Oundle, and touches briefly on Thrapston, both of which are gateway towns to the Forest (much of which now comes under the administrative district of East Northamptonshire). As both towns have been well-documented, this book also turns the spotlight on several lesser-known villages in the area, among them: Apethorpe, Benefield, Brigstock, Fotheringhay, Kingscliffe, Lowick, Nassington, Southwick, Sudborough, Wansford (now in Cambridgeshire), Wadenhoe, Woodnewton and Yarwell. Inevitably, it has not been possible to include all the villages of such a large area in this book; perhaps any omissions will be rectified in a later volume.

For architectural splendour, the area is unrivalled: it contains some of the finest churches in the county at Fotheringhay, Brigstock and Lowick. Among the great buildings are those of Oundle School, Lyveden New Bield, Southwick Hall, Apethorpe Hall (home of Sir Walter Mildmay, who was Chancellor of the Exchequer to Elizabeth I), Elton Hall, Fermyn Woods Hall, Drayton House, and the oldest continuously inhabited building in the county, the Prebendal Manor House at Nassington.

Sadly, much has been lost: the castles of Fotheringhay (the birthplace of Richard III and prison and place of execution for Mary Queen of Scots), Benefield, Titchmarsh, Thorpe Waterville (which saw action during the Wars of the Roses), and the royal manor house of Kingscliffe (a favourite residence of King John, Edward I and Edward II whilst on their hunting visits to the Forest). Today only Barnwell Castle and Woodcroft Castle remain to remind us of that era. Other losses include the medieval settlements of Churchfield, Hale, Perio, Lilford, Elmington, Armston, Papley and the great pottery-making complex of Lyveden.

Well-known names associated with the area include John Dryden (dramatist and Poet Laureate, born in Aldwincle); Robert Browne (founder of Congregationalism and a rector of Thorpe Achurch); William Law (religious writer, and benefactor of Kingscliffe, where he set up an almshouse and school, working to improve the lot of the poor with, amongst others, the sister of Edward Gibbon, author of *The Rise and Fall of the Roman Empire*); William Laxton (Master of the Grocers' Company and a Lord Mayor of London, who set up an almshouse and school in Oundle), and Nicholas Latham of Brigstock (who founded schools and almshouses in Oundle, Brigstock, Weekley and Barnwell). The authors George Eliot and Anthony Trollope stayed on various occasions at Lowick Rectory and D.J. Watkins-Pritchard, alias 'BB', lived at Sudborough.

Although the people, buildings, fashions, and life-styles of the area have either changed or disappeared, a lot still remains. A common spirit and sense of timelessness pervades the villages and the town of Oundle has preserved much of its past. A large network of footpaths and bridleways pattern the surrounding countryside and many forest-related crafts are returning, as visits to Lower Benefield, Woodnewton and Brigstock will show.

This book gives us a long-overdue glimpse into the area's past, bringing it alive once again via pictures that were meant to be seen and shared and are our heritage.

Peter Hill
April 1997

One
Oundle

An engraving of The Talbot Inn, Bury Street (now New Street), made during the Regency Period.

New Street at the turn of the century, showing The Talbot Inn (left foreground) and The Turks Head (to the left of the horse-and-carriage).

The Talbot Inn, New Street, 1903. This famous coaching inn stands on the site of a much earlier hostelry and was formerly known as The Tabret. Much of the present building dates from 1626. Some of the window casements are said to have come from Fotheringhay Castle when it was dismantled after standing in a state of disrepair for several years.

The Talbot Inn, from the courtyard. A building to the right of the carriage has a datestone of 1776, above which three tuns (the symbol of the J. Smith Brewery) are depicted. This came from the old brewery building in North Street when it was demolished.

One of Oundle's former pubs, The White Lion, *c.* 1890. It was built in 1641 and stood in North Street.

Another of the town's former pubs, The Anchor Inn, in St Osyth's Lane, 1909. This distinctive pub was rebuilt in 1637 and stood on this site for many years. The fine adjoining buildings have now been demolished and today a foodstore stands in their place.

A rare view of Inkerman Place, or Yard, 1908. Twenty four houses stood here using paraffin for lighting and even cooking until as late as 1960. The site was off West Street, at the Jesus Church end.

Excitement in West Street, in the midst of General Election fever, 1906. The crowd appears to be gathering outside the shop of the well known town printer and stationer, H. Markham, in expectation of some news.

Do not wait until the next
COAL SHORTAGE
But Buy your Supplies NOW
— FROM —

W. McMichael & Son,
Coal and Coke Merchants,
WEST STREET, OUNDLE.

Special Quotations for Large Quantities.
:: :: Truck Loads to any Station. :: ::

'Phone 15.   Also at Wellingborough and Rushden.

Trade advertisement for W. McMichael & Son, coal merchant. This serves as a reminder of this once commonly-used fuel, in the days before central heating. Note the low digit telephone number!

Coulson's the saddler's, New Street, *c*. 1900.

Another well-known sight in West Street was Charles Claridge's grocery business, here seen in 1908. This building still serves as a shop. The former Vine public house can be seen to the right.

View towards Jericho, from the corner of North Street, 1919. The shop on the corner is now Owen and Hartleys.

Repairs to Oundle Bridge, January 1912. The repair programme of this long eleven arch structure continued until 1914. The reason for rebuilding it is all too evident from this scene of a flood.

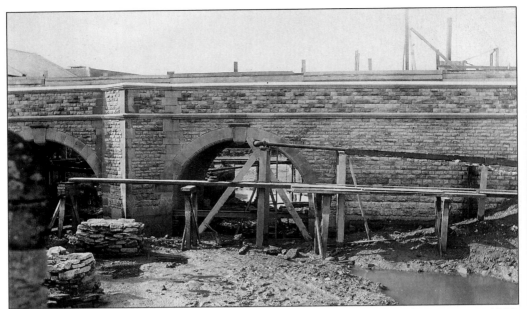

Another view of the bridge under repair, 1912. A stone tablet found in the parapet in 1835, during repairs, reads: 'In the yere of our Lord 1570 thes arches wer borne doune by the waters extremytie. In the yere of our Lord 1571 they wer bulded agayne with lyme and stonne. Thanks be to God'.

St Ann's in the Grove Infant School, Queen Victoria Diamond Jubilee, 1897. The school was built in 1862 and part of the building survives today (with a diamond shaped datestone) on the corner of Benefield Road and Milton Road (formerly Milton Lane) next to the Drill Hall. Today, the site is occupied by the auto repair firm of Francis and Marshall.

The British School, 1895. The school was built in 1843 behind West Street, at the Jesus Church end of the town. The building has since been converted into private accommodation.

A Sunday school group at St Ann's in the Grove, 1890s. The flags indicate some kind of celebration, which has not been identified.

'Welcome to the Grocer's Company', 13 September 1883. A triumphal arch was erected to mark the opening of the new Oundle School (that is, the Grocer's Company School) building, the Cloisters (pictured right). This marked the beginning of a period of expansion of the school in the vicinity of New Street over the next few years, during which many existing buildings, such as those seen here on the left-hand-side of the road, disappeared. Amongst these were the T. Barnes Brewery and yard. The new School House opened on this site in 1887.

The seventeenth-century White Hart Inn, New Street, 1873. It was demolished between November 1880 and the early months of 1881 to provide part of the site for the Cloisters.

The Victoria Cinema, West Street, 1953, four years after its opening in March 1949. Its opening was of historic interest, being the first municipal cinema in England. It closed in 1963.

The Cloisters as they appeared in 1903. The railings disappeared during the Second World War, when a desperate national appeal was made to collect metal for the manufacture of arms.

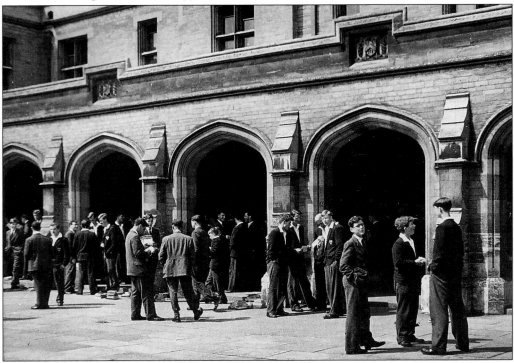

The Cloisters of Oundle School, July 1958.

The School House, New Street, c. 1903. To the right of the building can be seen part of the Red Lion public house, purchased by the school in 1906 as part of its expansion programme. The arched doorway with a panel depicting the arms of the Grocer's Company was later moved to the other end of the building and can seen in the next photograph.

The School House, 1908. In the following year, The Turk's Head public house (pictured here as the building with the wide square doorway) and the shop of the plumber and decorator C. Curtis were purchased by the school. These buildings, together with an adjoining butcher's shop, were demolished at a later date.

Folkestone Cottages, New Street, a few months before the thirty-year-old houses were demolished to make room for the main building of Oundle School Great Hall in 1908.

Oundle School Great Hall, 1958. The wings were added to the main building in 1910.

Assembly in the Great Hall, July 1958.

A visit by Benefield School to Oundle School, 1910. The headmaster (pictured centre) is Mr Algernon Pike and behind him to the left is the Revd Richardson.

A visit by Field Marshal Bernard Montgomery to Oundle School in October, 1947.

The cricket pavilion of Oundle School, July 1958.

A visit by the Queen Mother to Oundle School, May 1976.

Smith's Brewery. The brewery was set up in 1775 and lasted until 1962, far outlasting its two rivals, the Union Brewery (1835/53) and the Anchor Brewery (1854/1904). The building, which stood on the corner of Black Pot Lane and North Street, was demolished in 1967.

Oundle Station, *c.* 1897.

The old post and sorting office, corner of East Road and St Osyth's Lane, *c.* 1909. Note the new-looking Edward VII pillar box.

The old Oundle police station, corner of Stoke Hill and Mill Road, 1905. The building in the foreground was built in 1877 and housed the station and cells, with the magistrates court adjoining in Mill Road.

Construction of gas storage cylinders in East Road, 1890. The site stood close to where the football ground is today.

View towards West Street from the Town Hall and Market Place, at the turn of the century.

Three businesses in West Street, c. 1920: E. Wright (ironmonger), D.W. Redhead (baker, confectioner, wine and spirit dealer) and A. Lloyd (draper).

A lady from Glapthorn, en route to Oundle. Taken on the Glapthorn Road, *c.* 1895.

West Street, *c.* 1910, outside the entrance to Danfords, which stood opposite the Congregational chapel, now the Stahl Theatre. The archway is still a prominent feature of the street.

An unknown group of Oundle transport enthusiasts, *c.* 1913. It is intriguing to think that a race might be about to start!

A group of Oundle people enjoy a last picnic of the season at Polebrook Corner, October 1915.

RIVER NENE OUNDLE

Boating on the Nene, summer 1908.

Relaxing on a Sunday afternoon outside Oundle Boat House, 4 August 1914.

THE OUNDLE OPERATIC SOCIETY.

Affiliated to the   *N.A.O. & D. Association.*

VICTORIA HALL – OUNDLE.

The Tenth Annual Production.

THE SOCIETY presents

"The Belle of Brittany"

A Charming Musical Play in Two Acts.

Book by Leedham Bantock and P. J. Barrow.   Lyrics by Percy Greenbank.   Music by Howard Talbot.

TUESDAY, FEBRUARY 8th, 1927, for Five Nights, at 7.30 p.m.

Matinée on Saturday, February 12th, at 2.30 p.m.

Prices : Tuesday—3/-, 2/-, 1/-, 6d. (including tax).   Wednesday, Thursday, Friday, and Saturday
Matinée.—5/-, 3/6, 2/4, 1/2 (including tax).   Saturday Evening—5/9, 4/6, 3/- (including tax).

One of the many productions of the former Oundle Operatic Society, at the Victoria Hall in West Street, 1927.

Oundle Operatic Society, the cast of *Tom Jones*, January 1921.

May Day, Milton Road, c. 1910. The May Queen is believed to have been Bessie Palmer. The use of streamers attached to the Maypole was a Victorian idea, part of its sanitisation of the old ceremony which had existed since pagan times. The May Day song of the time consisted of eight or nine verses. In the Oundle version from 1890 until the First World War, the first five verses were of a religious nature, beginning:

> 'Remember us poor Mayers, all
> And now we do begin,
> To lead our lives in righteousness
> For fear we die in Sin.'

The next three verses bring in a more pagan, or natural, flavour, beginning:

> 'Oh we've been rambling all the night
> And most part of the day,
> And now we've come to see you all
> With a branch of our sweet May.'

The song would be sung whilst calling at houses in the town.

An Empire Pageant by children of the National School, 1893. Also known as a 'church school', this was one of Oundle's three earliest schools for the town's children and was founded in 1842. It still stands at the Glapthorn Road end of Milton Road and is known today as Oundle Primary School.

A card sent by an Oundle man who had enlisted in the army with other local recruits, July 1915.

Proclamation of King George V, after his father's death in May 1910. Compare the formality of this scene with that of the next photograph, taken a year later.

Celebrating the coronation of George V, near the Market Hall, 22 June 1911. Note the number of boaters – a long-lasting fashion item since 1885. The streets are festooned with 'God Save the King' banners and bunting.

Glapthorn Road Hospital. The picture shows just a fraction of this massive complex. For the first ninety years, the main block was the Oundle Union Workhouse. It became a hospital in the 1930s. A long fight to keep it open failed and it was demolished in the 1970s.

These buildings on the corner of Benfield Road, opposite Jesus Church, stood derelict for a long time after a fire destroyed them during building work. One of the town's many public houses had once stood on the corner, but in its final days the building was a grocer's shop run by E.O. Roberts.

Two
Yarwell and Wansford

Yarwell Mill, 1911. One of many mills set up along the River Nene. A mill has stood here for centuries and the present building dates from 1839. The neighbouring mill-house is from the 1730s. Although no longer functioning it is part of a leisure area for boating and caravans.

Yarwell, looking towards the main street of the village from Nassington Road and Wansford Road, 1910.

Yarwell, centre of the main street, c. 1911. The girl on the left is Doris Steel and the boy on the right is Arthur Simmonds.

Yarwell. Arthur Simmons again, further along the street, this time on a horse named 'Captain'. This photograph was sent to the young man when he was a soldier fighting in the trenches during the First World War.

Yarwell, Sun Dial House, 1922. The building dates back to the seventeenth century and was formerly one of the village bakeries. Victorian ovens still stand at the rear of the house. It is named after the sundial which stands on a pillar in the garden.

Yarwell, at the crossroads at the top of the main street, 1910. The pond has long been filled in. Today a bus shelter stands on the site. The sign is pointing left to Old Sulehay, where one of the old Rockingham Forest lodges stands. The present building dates from 1642. The two men are walking towards Wansford.

The Northamptonshire Regiment marching along the road from Yarwell to Wansford, c. 1919.

Mrs Harriet Peach at the doorway of her cottage in the main street, Yarwell, *c.* 1910.

Yarwell, Keeper's Lodge. This fine old building stood close to the Wansford Road for many years and was part of the Westmorland Estate. It was burnt down in the 1990s.

The thirteenth-century church of Mary Magdalene, Yarwell, 1896, four years after the thatched roof was replaced with tiles. Inside the church is an eighteenth-century chest tomb to a prosperous merchant and alderman of London, Humphrey Bellamy, inscribed with a decorative 'wild man'.

Yarwell Football Team, c. 1920. Back row, left to right: M. Simmons, G. Gilbert, C. Longfoot, R. Ellis, J. Peach, G. Wass, A. Sharpe, H. Andrews. Front row, left to right: J. Hubbard, W. Hailstone, C. Simmons, J. Booth, -?-.

Yarwell, The Angel Inn, August 1902. A flag is draped from an upstairs window as part of the celebrations for Edward VII's coronation, which was delayed for two months because of an appendicitis operation. In the foreground, left to right are: Sid Clipsham, Mr Kidd, a decorated Hackney horse being held by its owner, Mr E. West. The small man by the pub window is Mr W. Peach, the tall man with the straw boater left of the door is Bert Mould and looking out of the window is Jack Andrews. Wilfred West is sitting on the donkey which is held by his brother, James. Seated in the middle are Mr and Mrs Brown, with their daughters, Mary and Hilda. The publican at the time was John Allen.

Yarwell, The Angel Inn, 1935. Saturday lunchtime, after work has finished. Left to right are: Sid Hill, Charlie Hudson, A. Simmons (one of the last-known professional mowers of hay and corn), Edward Briggs (farm foreman and horsekeeper at nearby Manor Farm), Mr and Mrs Sid Clipsham (landlord and lady of The Angel), W. Simmons (grandson of A. Simmons) and three little girls: Joyce and Lucy Clipsham and Jean Wass. At one time, the village boasted two other pubs: The Fox Inn and The Mason's Arms.

Wansford, The Old Mermaid public house, 1912. The photograph was taken from outside the church, and the road to its right was the original A1, now the Old North Road. The pub was later known as The New Mermaid. Like its two near neighbours, The Marquis of Granby and The Black Swan, it no longer exists as a public house.

Wansford Bridge, February 1914. An Eddison Roller has crashed into a wall of the bridge, causing damage to the masonry. This must have caused some disruption to the erstwhile A1, even though the motor car had not yet begun to dominate the road.

Wansford Bridge, c. 1910, looking towards the Northamptonshire part of the village. The fine old bridge with its ten arches and pedestrian refuges has graffiti dating from as early as 1577 on its stonework. The southern portion of the bridge was rebuilt in 1795, after ice had severely damaged the surface making it impassable by traffic.

View from the Bridge, Wansford.

View from Wansford Bridge, *c.* 1927. This is looking at the Huntingdonshire side of the village, with the famous Haycock Inn on the left. The River Nene marked the boundary between the Soke of Peterborough (then Northamptonshire) and Huntingdonshire. An inscribed metal marker still stands on the bridge. Both parts of the village are now in Cambridgeshire.

Wansford, carnival time, *c.* 1912. Little is known about this intriguing photograph, and what exactly is going on in it!

Three
Apethorpe, Woodnewton and Fotheringhay

Apethorpe, c. 1903. A group of family and friends pose in a field for this photograph, taken after a wedding. The picture, although slightly marred by the restless baby, is still very fine.

Apethorpe, c. 1910. The last of the village post offices, dating from the seventeenth century is no longer used. The scene has hardly changed today. Even traffic seems to have little effect on the peaceful atmosphere. Note the soft cycle-scarred surface of the main road. The church of St Leonard stands in the background. This is a fine building with one of the most elaborate early seventeenth-century tombs in the county, the Mildmay tomb and, from the same period, some rare stained-glass depicting biblical scenes.

Apethorpe, 1906. Many of the houses in the village are still thatched and have quaint-sounding names. This photograph was taken from the gates of Apethorpe Hall, and shows the old post office jutting out at the far end of the street and a row of thatched cottages, now demolished, on the immediate left.

Apethorpe, the old stable block of Apethorpe Hall, *c.* 1920. The original section of the Hall was built in 1480 by Sir Guy Wolston and parts were added by Sir Walter Mildmay and the Westmorland family. Queen Elizabeth I stayed here in 1566 and James I found it particularly pleasant, staying five times between 1605/19.

Woodnewton, Hill Tree Corner, *c.* 1908. Taken from the Fotheringhay Road, looking towards Main Street and right towards the Nassington Road. Today, the small green on the right has a colourful wooden sign for the village, made by a traditional craftsman who works in the village.

Woodnewton, *c*. 1914, looking down Main Street from opposite the church.

Barfield's Carpentry and Carriage Building firm in Woodnewton, *c*. 1919. This was a well-known industry in the area with a reputation for quality products. Joe Barfield, the owner, is in the wheelchair, and a fine assortment of wheels and timber can be seen in the yard next to The White Swan pub.

Fotheringhay, church of St Mary the Virgin. This fine photograph, dating from the turn of the century, is taken from the banks of the River Nene. A castle stood opposite this place until the early seventeenth century. Here, Richard III was born in 1452 and Mary Queen of Scots was executed in 1587.

Fotheringhay. As above, from the front gates, 1902. This church is but a shadow of its former self. A large portion of the building was lost when the religious college attached to it was dismantled in the years following the Dissolution of the Monastaries in the sixteenth century. Memorials to members of the York family can be seen in the church.

Fotheringhay. May Day celebrations in the 1950s. This is Castle Farm Cottage, near the narrow eighteenth-century road bridge which spans the Nene.

Eaglethorpe, Warmington, *c.* 1910. Once known as Mill End, little of the original village remains today. The photograph shows Eaglethorpe House, part of which dates from the late sixteenth century. A door and frame from Fotheringhay Castle were later incorporated in the building. A superb seventeenth-century circular dovecote and the old mill lie close by.

Four

Nassington

Station Road looking towards Yarwell, with Church Street leading off to the left, *c.* 1910.

Station Road, summer 1912. A little further along the road from the previous photograph. There is still no traffic or pavements!

Station Road, looking towards the village from the railway track, winter 1894.

Station Road, 26 August 1912. The Nene has burst its banks and flooded the street. In fact, in this photograph, the street looks like an extension of the river! Such a sight was not unusual in villages near the Nene and Welland.

Church Street, *c*. 1910. The houses on the right were known as 'The Barracks'. The sign of The Three Mill Bills can be seen on the left. This, together with the nearby Three Horseshoes and The Plough, no longer exists as a public house. The barn further along the street is now a house.

Nassington Manor House, rear view, 1912. This partly early-sixteenth-century building was associated with the Wolston family of Apethorpe for many years, and has a fine oriel window on the side facing Woodnewton Road. Next door is the oldest continuously inhabited house in the county, the Prebendal Manor House, which dates in part from the thirteenth century, and which housed important church officials from Lincoln Diocese.

Church Street, the police house (left), 1910. Notice the sign above the door showing the rose of Northamptonshire.

A row of seventeenth-century thatched cottages, standing opposite the church. Many houses like these in the village were built with unusually thick walls, some of them of up to three feet.

Church Street, The Three Horseshoes, 1914. The landlord at the time was Elias Knight, who also ran a blacksmith's. He had moved from Yarwell in 1910 to run the public house and moved back again in 1917 to work for his brother Tom, who was a wheelwright and blacksmith at the railway end of Nassington. Left to right: Mrs Fanny Knight, Beryl Knight (her daughter), Mr Knight with baby, Tom Knight, Claude Knight, Miriam Knight and Clarrie Knight.

Back garden of The Queen's Head, Station Road, 1908. Among those pictured are: Hettie Scotney (centre), Mr Scotney (far right) a retired police inspector of Oundle who took over the pub, his wife, seated next to him, and Grandma Dixon (far left). The fishing trip looks like it was thirsty work, judging by the number of bottles lying around!

Members and friends of the Hodson family, pictured in 1910. Among those pictured in the back row are: Tom Hodson (with the gun) who was a keen fisherman and Mr Egerton (centre) who was a ferry captain on a visit from London. The smiling lady in the large hat, who is leaning forward, is Polly Hodson. The Hodson children grew up at Baxter's Barn.

Members of the Freestone family in the garden of their house, opposite Mould the butcher's in Station Road, 1900.

The church of St Mary and All Saints, with the old vicarage (which was later demolished) to the side of the entrance gate, 1878.

Repair work on the steeple of the church, which was struck by lightning on 14 May 1905, causing considerable damage.

Decorated house, Church Street, June 1911. When George V was crowned, houses were decorated with bunting, flags and flowers, as part of the celebrations. This was also the year that National Insurance contributions were introduced and MPs were paid for the first time!

May Day, Nassington School, 1920. Among those pictured are: Florence Taylor, Maurice Rowles, Kathleen Barr and Edith Hall.

Miss Annie Ireson on her decorated bicycle, *c. 1922.* Decorated bicycle events were popular at annual garden shows and church fete days in the first quarter of the century.

Nassington was always proud of its annual flower festival. A procession makes its way along Station Road, with a relatively new addition – the car – *c. 1920.*

A procession heading along Station Road during a special event, *c.* 1920. This is a curious picture, featuring elements of Plough Monday and May Day celebrations. Note, in particular, the 'Jack in the Green' figure, with blackened face and top hat, a feature of chimney sweeps who traditionally acted in this role.

Peterborough League Division Three Shield Winners, Nassington Football Team, 1934. Back row, left to right: George Mould, Sam Fenn, Reg Black, Fred Briggs, Stan Black, Ken Lock. Middle row, left to right: Dick Black, Dennis Leigh, George Bailey, Charles Black, Reg Chambers and Mr Thurston. Front row, left to right: Bert Jackson, Fred Cairns, Jim Broughton, Frank Barr and Jack Crane.

Fulbrook Farm, c. 1927. George White stands in the centre, with his brother Jack (right), who later became police chief of Hong Kong.

Crowson's Wood Yard, in the late 1890s. Robert and Albert Crowson made good quality farm gates, ladders, pegs, stakes and 'sheep trays' which were much in demand in the area. The yard stood next to the Congregational chapel in Station Road.

Re-roofing and converting the former Congregational chapel which had been used since 1839. At the time of this photograph a new one had been erected close by, next to The Queen's Head.

This rare photograph was taken outside the old rectory in Church Street during a summer in the mid 1870s. Road workers face the water pump and use the water to sprinkle on the road for laying the dust.

George Mould, butcher, pictured outside his shop in Station Road, with his wife and Barbara Freestone, *c.* 1947. Mr Mould, known affectionately as 'Uncle George', gave many lads in the village their first taste of work, by letting them help him make sausages, prepare the slaughterhouse, and look after the ponies and carts. He was also a keen bandsman and formed the very popular Nassington Band.

Joseph Scotney, butcher and landlord of The Queen's Head, Station Road, *c.* 1919. The shop adjoined the pub. He was also a breeder of Airedale terriers, which he exhibited at dog shows in the region.

The watch and clock repairer, Oakley Ireson, on his belt-driven BSA motorcycle with passenger and sidecar. He was much in demand in the area for his skills and his house in Station Road was described as 'an Aladdin's cave of interesting timepieces'. As well as being an expert signwriter and photographer, he also played and taught piano, violin and banjo.

Nassington Quarry, running from near Sulehay, was nearly a mile in length and up to sixty feet deep. It can still be seen from Bedford Purlieus.

Ransomes and Rapier W170 dragline in action at Nassington Quarry. It operated between 1939 and 1969. The quarry was worked by the Nassington and Barrowden Mining Company for its deposits of iron ore.

Quarrymen at Nassington Quarry, *c.* 1947.

A boring machine operated by Bill Codman and Sid Hill, pictured here greasing the machine. The jib was fifty feet high.

'Jacks Green', one of two engines used at the Nassington Quarry, the other being 'Ring Haw'. Both engines were named after local woods. The driver is Jimmy Hopkins.

Fire at Nassington Station, 9 October 1912. Although one side of the station was destroyed before the private steam engine from Elton arrived on the scene, the engine managed to limit the damage caused by the fire.

Nassington Station, dismantling in progress after the closure of the station in 1957.

Five

Kingscliffe

Park Street, looking towards the village centre, *c.* 1910. Two public houses can be seen in this picture: The Wheatsheaf, run by Charles Sharpe, on the right, and The Red Lion Inn, run by Tom Richardson, in the distance on the left. Of the original nine pubs, only The Cross Keys in West Street survives today.

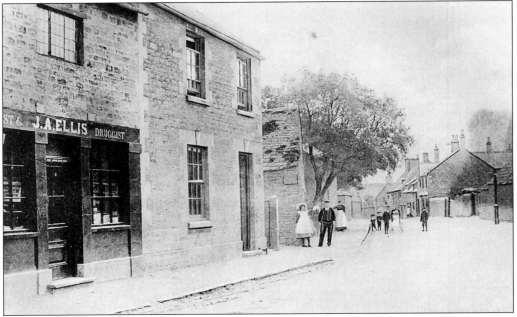

Park Street, looking towards the church, the steeple of which can be seen above the houses on the far right. Much of the scene is recognisable today, including the distinctive shopfront of J.A. Ellis, the chemist, which is now a home. The small house standing to the left of this couple has long since vanished.

Park Street, near the junction with West Street and Bridge Street, *c.* 1912. Thorpe's almshouses, built in 1668, can be seen at the top of the hill.

Bridge Street, King's Cliffe.

Bridge Street, *c.* 1906. Another of the village's former pubs, The Golden Ball, stands on the right, beyond the Edward VII Coronation Memorial, which was erected in the summer of 1902.

Bridge Street, looking towards West Street, *c.* 1904. The shop on the corner of Hall Hill (centre left) is still used today, as a butcher's and post office.

West Street, looking towards the centre of the village, *c.* 1910. The Congregational church, built in 1846, stands on the right. On the opposite side of the road is a bakery, which still exists today.

West Street, *c.* 1906, at the junction with what is now known as Forest Approach. The original post office stands on the left-hand corner and another of the village's pubs, The Turner's Arms (an acknowledgement of the village's fame as a woodturning centre), stands on the right. A bracket which held the pub sign can still be seen today.

West Street, with a view towards the Blatherwycke road, *c.* 1906. Although the shop on the right is no longer there, the building is still recognisable.

View from the railway embankment above the village, with Station Approach in the foreground, *c*. 1912. The hedged area is now a housing estate. The spire of the church is just visible in the distance, on the right.

KINGSCLIFFE CHURCH

The church of All Saints and St James, *c*. 1908. The twelfth-century tower and thirteenth-century spire are, unusually, positioned in the centre of the building, which was used by Cromwell's troops as stables during the Civil War and contains relics from part of the church at Fotheringhay.

Kingscliffe Station, 1920. The station closed down in 1966.

A 55 Flying Squadron Mustang and the Operations Block of the USAAF airbase at Kingscliffe. This was one of a cluster of bases set up in the Oundle area during the Second World War. Kingscliffe was the smallest, and was used by the 20th Fighter Group from August 1943.

First Lieutenant, Thomas A. 'Snake' Hanzo, assistant operations officer, 1942.

A visit to the airfield by Anthony Eden, Secretary of State for War and the future Prime Minister.

Pictured in the first-aid jeep are Ina Bacon and Eleanor Rogers. During an outbreak of rickets in Kingscliffe, the base gave crates of much-needed vitamin C, in the form of oranges, to the local school. There was such a large quantity that they were distributed to other schools in the Oundle area.

A group of flyers. The men flew in P36 Lightnings and later the superbly effective P51 Mustangs, on bomber escort duty. Despite considerable success, the base lost a total of 132 aircraft by the end of the war.

First Lieutenant Ken Schons, with his aeroplane, nicknamed 'The Virgin'.

The Roosevelt Bar. The free drinks must certainly have been popular! There was a lot of entertainment at the base, and Glen Miller, the famous US bandleader, played his last date here before his plane went missing en route to France in December 1944.

Six
Around Southwick

The west side of Southwick Hall, May 1880. This partly fourteenth-century building has a fine vaulted undercroft, north stair turret and ornate chimney tops.

The south side of Southwick Hall, 1890s. A horse-and-carriage can be seen outside. A Gothic door was added to the building after this picture was taken.

St Mary's church, *c.* 1870, with rounded Georgian windows in the nave, which were later replaced by mock Gothic windows.

The church from the street entrance, *c.* 1900.

The Capron family outside Southwick Grange, *c.* 1908.

View of the main street, looking towards the church, early 1900s. The sign and porch of the thatched Shukburgh Arms public house can be seen on the right. A former public house, The Bill and Hatchet, can be seen with its shutters in the foreground. This building has since been demolished.

The former grocery shop of V. Hudson (now Church Cottage), opposite the church, 1920s. The thatched roof and grassed area have now disappeared.

The Southwick Red Cross group, outside Southwick Hall, 10 Jan 1940, with the Duchess of Gloucester. Left to right: Ethel Burton, Maria ?, Roy Jackson, Mr Whitwell, Mrs Capron, the Duchess of Gloucester, -?-, Miss Gill, Ada Harris, Lady Ethel Wickham, and Mrs Fosskit.

Mr and Mrs G. Capron and family enjoying a Sunday afternoon stroll in the countryside around Southwick, August 1913.

A War Weapons fundraising group, wearing a variety of costumes and supported by a range of accessories, outside Southwick Hall during the Second World War.

A summer party for the villagers in the grounds of Southwick Hall, 3 August 1913.

One of the teams of Glapthorn Cricket Club, 1950s.

Morehay, *c.* 1919. The picture shows the start of a ploughing match – a popular event in the pre-tractor era. One of the distinctive, long-lived 'Druid Oaks' can be seen in the background. In medieval times, Morehay was one of three extra-parochial areas of the Forest used for royal hunting.

Seven
Benefield

Cricket at Benefield, *c.* 1905. The cricket pavilion was situated between the two villages of Upper and Lower Benefield. The man in the straw hat on the right is Sir Charles Gunning, a local dignitary.

Ladies Cricket at Benefield, 1902. It must have been quite difficult playing in long skirts! Notice what seems to be the original method of bowling underarm .

Lower Benefield, looking towards the village from Causin Way (Brigstock Road) at the turn of the century. Causin Way, like nearby Harley Way, is one of two surviving ancient tracks leading from Oundle to Brigstock.

Benefield School, Causin Way, 1902. The school was built in 1820 for 110 children. To encourage good and regular attendance, sums ranging from a penny to threepence were awarded to those pupils meeting targets.

Benefield School, 1902. Mr Algernon Pike, left, was headmaster of the school for many years and was considered to be one of the finest organists ever heard, making the church organ 'sing'. A strict disciplinarian, he was also widely respected as a fair and helpful man.

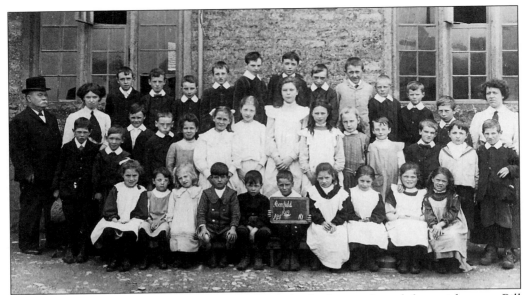

Benefield School, 1912. Among those pupils in the back row, from left to right, are: Bill Durrant, Billy Singlehurst, Charles Durral, Percy Knapp, Dick Nichols, Jack Morehen, Billy Tilley, and Miss Folkard (teacher). Centre, left to right: Mr Pike (headmaster), teacher (unknown), Arthur Fox, George Pywell, Billy Freer, Walter Fellower, Dolly Gilby, May Currall, Anne Bosworth, Dolly Currall, Anne Swan, Francis Northern, Grace Davis, - Durrant, Tonio Lorenzo, Fred Pywell. In the front row are, left to right: Mary Welsh, Grace Davis, Norma Northern, Billy Palanti, Sam Gilby, Herbert Fellowes (holding the slate), -?-, Maggie Plowright, Sheila West, Violet Freer.

The school in the 1950s, now buttressed and disused. Today the building is used as the village hall. Passing by, on the tractor, are Bill and Stan Druce, members of a family long-connected with Benefield.

Albert Pywell at Hatfield Farm, Upper Benefield, in 1944, with his Clydesdale horse, Pat. Standing to his left, with a bicycle, is Ralph Plowright.

Main Street, Upper Benefield, 1905. The Wheatsheaf Inn, run at this time by Sarah Carley, stands on the far right, with the Glapthorn Road to the left. Charles Parker, the wheelwright, is standing at the entrance to his workshop yard.

As above, looking in the opposite direction towards Weldon, *c.* 1910. In medieval times the village was known as Uppthorpe, or Overthorpe, to distinguish it from Benefield, which is now known as Lower Benefield.

Further along Main Street, 1912, after a fire which had been started by sparks from a threshing machine passing through the village. The roof of the house was later rebuilt, with Collyweston tiles. The thatched cottage behind the cyclists no longer exists.

Ploughing in Banty Ground, *c.* 1913. The main road lies to the right. Pictured are Smiler, Kit, Polly, and Bonny, with William Pywell at the plough. Mr Pywell's son, Albert, is with Polly, who every morning would take milk to Corby Station and bring back the empty churns.

Road maintenance men, Lower Benefield, at the turn of the century, looking along the main street in the direction of Oundle. The cart with its sacks of gravel is inscribed 'Russell'. Note the wheelbarrow, rake and spade for resurfacing the road. Today, a phone box is situated between the two houses in the foreground.

Lower Benefield, looking from the Oundle end of the main road, *c.* 1920.

As above, but further down the hill, at the turn of the century. Mr Jinks, the sexton, and his wife, are standing close to the shade of the butcher's shop which was run by William Chapman for many years.

The estate yard, Glapthorn Road, 1920. This operates today as a woodcraft centre.

Brook House, Glapthorn Road, 1910. This building, pictured on the left, has since been extended.

Lower Benefield, 1950s. The shop of J. Cheney, the butcher, can be seen on the right. It would be dangerous to take sheep along the road at this point today, with cars racing around the bend!

Benefield Guides outside Biggin Hall, in the 1930s.

May Day, 1919. In the foreground, to the left, are: Harry Pywell (holding the scroll of the May proclamation), Habo Pywell, -?-, the May Queen. Among those on the right are Lea Swann, Aubrey Clark, Tom Goodman, Harold Currall, Fred Bettles and Stan Bettles.

May Day in later years. Left to right are: Laura Dixon, Helen Gibbs, -?-, -?-, Margaret Dixon, with flowers in her hair, -?-, Phyllis Martin and Winnie Osbond. The two parts of Benefield never joined forces for the May Day celebrations, preferring to have separate processions within their own area.

Benefield Ladies Choir, 1940s. Back row, left to right: D. Bullas, Mrs Pearson, Winnie Osborne, Amy Northen, Florrie Currall. Middle row, left to right: Jessie Streather, Mrs Brudenell, Mrs Linda Pywell, Mrs Louie Wright. Front row, left to right: K. Freeman, M. Bosworth, H. Spendlove, Mary Fletcher, Jessie Spendlove, J. Bullas, and N. Butcher. Their 'test piece' was the Allelujah Chorus from Handel's Messiah.

Deenethorpe Airfield, 12 January 1945. The last of the USAAF bases in the Oundle area to be set up, in October 1943. It was used by the 401st Bombardment Group, with its Flying Fortresses, and distinguished itself in action, at the cost of ninety five lost aircraft by the end of the war. The airstrips today are used for private flying lessons. A memorial to the men who flew from the base stands along the Benefield-Weldon road.

Eight
Brigstock

'The Bullring', *c.* 1923. This was a circular area of grass on the corner of Church Lane and Park Walk.

St Andrew's church, 1904. This is one of the most distinctive churches in the county, part-Saxon, with a semi-circular stair turret similar to that seen at Brixworth.

Jabez Rowell, fellmongers, 1898. Note the pile of animal skins in the corner. The site stood beside Harpers Brook for many years, but was later demolished, and is now occupied by a residential home for the elderly.

Mill House, 1905. This part eighteenth-century building was last worked in 1910, but the wheel and gears are still intact today.

The Manor House. This was formerly a royal hunting lodge for monarchs visiting Rockingham Forest, and was particularly favoured by King John, who on one particular occasion held court here. In the twentieth century, it was used as a convalescent home for film stars!

The Old Three Cocks, High Street, 1926. The entrance of this former coaching inn has changed somewhat since this picture was taken. The Old Three Cocks and The Green Dragon are the only two of thirteen pubs still in operation. During the war, the American film star Clark Gable, who was stationed at the USAAF airbase at Polebrook, had a room for entertaining here.

View towards the Sudborough Road from the corner of Grafton Road, 1902.

'The Matchbox'. This was built between 1872 and 1873 by Wallis and Linnell, who set up other factories in the Rockingham Forest area for the production of clothing. The building was designed in this unique way, in order to let as much light in as possible. Today, it is used as an architects' office.

Working inside the Matchbox, 1955. Among the ladies at work on the machines are: Wendy Shiels (front left), Gwen Swan (front right) and Pam Wright and Rita Bailey behind.

Thomas Hector with some of his family, outside their cottage in Bridge Street, 1898. A member of a long-established local family, he had moved from Stanion to Brigstock 'New Town' in 1870, to raise a large family in the village. Left to right: Thomas, his daughter-in-law with her son Ted, Grace Hector, and Kathleen Hector.

This charming picture of three little schoolgirls was taken in 1915, in the garden of Latham School. From left to right are: Lois Starsmore, Gracy Hector and Rene Hector.

Brigstock Band, 1921. The photograph was taken outside Whitehall House, Park Walk. Back row, left to right: ? Seddon, Ben Smith, Harry Mayes, Harry Blades, Pearce Hector, Tom Hector, Clarence Hector, Herbert Abbott, Harry Blades snr., Ern Bell, Bern Hector, Charles Swan and Jack Hector. Front row, standing: Cyril Blades, Joe Swan, Jack Swan. Front row, sitting: Harry Hector, Bernard Hector (bandmaster), Archie Bell.

Corner of Park Walk and Grafton Road, 1905. The baby in the pram has been identified as Lesley Reeves.

The Market Cross, 1901. This dates from 1466 and is inscribed on its sides with the initials of various English queens from Elizabeth I to our present Elizabeth II. The market itself has long ceased to exist.

Bridge Street, looking towards Toseland's grocer's shop (now Druce's), 1946. The boys on the left are: Brian Starsmore, Walter Wise and John Wise. The girls on the right are: June Hawkins, Madge Gray, and Ruth Gray.

Bottom Bridge, 1880. This fine eighteenth-century bridge in Bridge Street, with its pedestrian sanctuary, now spans a grassy stretch with just a trickle of water flowing across it. Harpers Brook once flowed through its arches, before its course was diverted some years ago.

Looking towards The Syke and Cackle End, c. 1905. This picture was taken from the corner of Stable Hill, beside The Green Dragon. Cackle End is so-called because of all the local gossip that took place here whilst water was being drawn from the pump!

Timber about to be loaded onto drays, 1908. Trees were cut down slowly and laboriously with cross-cut saws and axes. There were no chain-saws in those days! Note the manner in which the bases have been fashioned.

Horses from Brigstock taking loads of timber via Causin Way to Benefield, *c.* 1900.

Fire at Hall Hill, 1956. The workhouse which formerly stood here was completely destroyed after a spark from a neighbouring chimney set fire to the thatched roof. Among those helping to stem the damage are Don Spencer (left of the ladder) and Wally Lettin (with the tray).

The Mace sisters outside their distinctively-styled house in the High Street, c. 1910. The Mace family were local builders and carpenters.

Tresham Lodge ('First Gate Lodge'), Causin Way, *c.* 1890. A wooden gate spans the road, in order to keep deer from the park from escaping. The lodge has been extended in recent years. A 'Second Gate Lodge' stood further along the road near Fermyn Woods Hall.

Staff outside Fermyn Woods Hall, during the 1890s. This stately building, originally known as Farming Woods Hall, started as a small deer park lodge in the fourteenth century. The earliest surviving parts of the present building are from the seventeenth century, including an inscribed gateway from nearby Lyveden Old Building.

Nine
Towards Thrapston

Stoke Doyle Rectory, *c.* 1910.

The lock gates, Wadenhoe, *c.* 1928. This part of the River Nene was a popular swimming area, if a little dangerous!

A group of children outside the old Wadenhoe South Lodge at the top of Church Street and Mill Lane, 1920s. This unusually shaped eighteenth-century building was one of two entrance lodges to Wadenhoe House. It was later extended.

Wadenhoe, The Cottage, a T-shaped building of the eighteenth century, and formerly the old Glebe House, at the corner of Church Street and Pilton Road, 1920s.

Wadenhoe, outside the old Glebe House, in
Church Street, 1929.

Wadenhoe, outside a barn, near the
corner of Church Street and Mill Lane,
1929.

Wadenhoe. Moving house in Main Street, 1920s. The house shown is next to the post office/shop. The chimney at the rear of the building is that of the washhouse, which is now demolished.

Lilford Hall, *c.* 1910. The building was for many years associated with the Powys family and dates from 1635. In the nineteenth century it was famous for its aviaries, which were created by Lord Lilford, president of the British Ornithologists Association. The village of Lilford and its church, St Peter's, were demolished when the estate was expanded in the 1770s.

Drayton House, 1921. The original parts of the house date back to the fourteenth and fifteenth centuries, but the main structure is of a much later date. The house was associated in medieval times with the De Vere family, later Earls of Oxford. It stands in splendid isolation, with a former deer park, between Lowick and Slipton.

The main entrance gates to Drayton House, 1921. There is a local tradition that if the clock ever strikes thirteen, the eagles on the gateposts will fly away!

Lowick, across the fields from Sudborough. This is a rare picture of the 'Lowick Oak', one of the great old trees of Rockingham Forest, which was blown down in a storm in 1968. It was ninety feet high and had an immense girth of twenty five feet. In the 1920s, twelve men held a dinner party inside the tree, complete with table!

John Cunnington, threshing-machine contractor and member of a large influential family in the Oundle/Thrapston area, who were engaged in such diverse industries as brewing, milling and butchery. He was instrumental in setting up the Oddfellows Hall in Thrapston.

119

Lowick. Mrs J. Cunnington and daughter, outside Vine Cottage, Robbs Lane, 1902.

Lowick, Church Row looking towards Sudborough, 1920.

Lowick, Drayton Road, c. 1924. The post office is visible on the left. The top of the beautiful lantern tower of the church of St Peter can be seen rising above the thatched house in the centre.

Lowick, Festival of Britain Celebrations, July 1951.

Sudborough, Manor Farm, 1950s. This is believed to be the oldest surviving house in the village, its original stone now encased in brick.

208. Sudborough, Main Street, 1910. The Vane Arms stands on the right. The cart loaded with wooden faggots in the background has come from Spencers, the timber merchants, at Brigstock.

Sudborough, looking towards Lowick, 1922. One of the village's old water pumps can be seen in the middle of the church wall on the right. The entrance to the old nineteenth-century school can be seen in the centre of the picture. The thatched cottages to its right have long since disappeared.

Sudborough, 1951. The thatched houses in the foreground were the oldest in the village. They stood close to the old school in the main street and acted as a meeting place for religious dissenters in earlier times.

123

Sudborough School May Day, 1940. This was a celebration with a difference. The May wreath is on the ground, taking second place to the banner, which reads: 'War Weapons Week. £900 Wanted From Sudborough. What Will You Give?'

Islip School, opposite the church in School Lane (formerly Church Lane), 1924. It was built in 1862, extended later that century, and closed in 1992.

King Edward Cottages, Thrapston

Islip. King Edward Cottages, Kettering Road. These lie opposite the partly sixteenth-century Woolpack Inn, and were built early in the reign of the newly-crowned king. They were occupied in 1903 by workers at the nearby Islip Furnaces. (The card should read Islip, for Thrapston lies on the other side of the 'Nine Arch Bridge' and the Nene river that separates the two settlements).

The grandstand at Thrapston Sports Ground, 1908. This was a very popular venue not just locally, but nationally, attracting large crowds from all over the country for various sporting events, including the Midland Cross Country. It no longer exists, as the site is now under water as a result of subsequent industrial sand and gravel extraction.

Aldwincle farmer, and captain of Thrapston Harriers, William Coales. This superb athlete was an Olympic medal winner in 1908, Midland Cross Country Champion, and winner of several important races in England. He is seen here in 1907 with some of his winners trophies, including that of the Three Mile Event at the Oval in South London.

Huntingdon Road, Thrapston, 1923. Little seems to have changed in the street, which is no longer the main (or only) route to Oundle. The railings have been replaced with newer ones. The only major change is the disappearance of the Institute (the small building partially obscured by the tree on the right).

South Terrace, Market Road, Thrapston, 1925. This view has changed considerably: the lower range of houses in the foreground have now disappeared, as have the two identical buildings seen at the end of the road. The houses in the middle are still recognisable, with a range of supporting wall ties at each gable end.

Thrapston Vicarage (or more correctly, the Rectory), Midland Road. This is the third of four vicarages in the town in the past hundred years. The others stand close by, or in the Oundle Road. Today it is a private house, and stands next to the now-deserted Smith and Grace's Engineering Works.

Acknowledgements

I would like to thank Oundle School, Oundle History Society, Reg Sutton, Toni Palenski, John Measures, The 20th Fighter Historical Group, Northamptonshire Record Office, Sue Paine, Willowbrook Local History Group, Audrey Singlehurst, Carl Hector, Tony Coales, Bridget Capron, Bill Richardson, Harry Pywell, Peter Hall, Ron Mears, Ann Lambert, Sarah Downes, and all the many unnamed individuals who kindly gave information, or who loaned photographs from their treasured family albums or collections, to be seen and shared by a wider audience. The work of local photographers, Oakley Ireson and A. Wright is also acknowledged. Without the contribution of all these people, this book would not have been possible. Every attempt has been made to contact copyright holders, and apologies are offered if any such ownership has not been acknowledged.